THE STORIES BEHIND MY SCARS

THULISILE P MBATHA

authorHOUSE

AuthorHouse™ UK
1663 Liberty Drive
Bloomington, IN 47403 USA
www.authorhouse.co.uk
Phone: UK TFN: 0800 0148641 (Toll Free inside the UK)
        UK Local: 02036 956322 (+44 20 3695 6322 from outside the UK)

Published by AuthorHouse 02/17/2021

ISBN: 978-1-6655-8612-2 (sc)
ISBN: 978-1-6655-8611-5 (e)

Print information available on the last page.

This book is printed on acid-free paper.

About the Author

My name is Thulisile Pearl Mbatha I am 17 years old. I was born on the 14 May 2003 in Mpumalanga. I currently live with my grandmother in Gauteng. I lost both my parents when I was very young. I have two older brothers. I suffer from Clinical depression; which I have had for 6 years, for the past 6 years I have been cutting myself. I have had a really rough childhood I was abused and bullied. So many times, I tired getting help but I always got judged because many people believed that people like me either have satanism or want attention. I began writing poems in 2016 which was a way for me to express my emotions. I don't always allow my depression to get the best of me. I love and care for everyone.

Contents

ॐ ॐ ॐ

10 Years

It's been ten years
    but
  it feels like 10 days!

It's been ten years
    since I
  last saw your smile,
heard your laughter!

It's been ten years
    but I
  still can't get over that you are
        gone forever!

Never to see you again, to
      create new memories
  together!

It's been ten years but I
     still can't put you
  in the past but rather in the present!

It's been ten years and
the memories we created
and shared still haunt!

It's been ten years and
I still miss you!

☙ ℬ ☙

64 Cuts

She broke her record,
　　she out numbered
her competition!

Her 64 cuts made her
　　smile wilder than anyone
　　　　has ever made
her smile!

The dripping of blood from
　　each cut,
　made her body feel lighter!

The numbness of the pain
　　gave her so much
　　　　satisfaction!

Her fresh wounds made
　　　her, realize
　this is her life!

Her 64 cuts were the
　　best thing
　that had happened to her!

A Mess

My life is a mess!
Why do I have to dwell?
in the future, when
I can dwell in the past!

My past is my future,
it keeps me alive!
My future has become a
misty path!

I have survived dwelling in,
my sorrow and tears!
I have survived all my cuts
and heartbreaks!

My life does not move on,
from the past, but,
stays in the past instead!

My life may be a mess but,
at least I am still,
living!

I may have wanted to
commit suicide so many times!
but every time I failed I
came out stronger!

I may be a sixteen-year-old
but
I have more scars that all have a
story than
        a tree that is over 100 years!

My life is a mess but life has also taught
        me how to survive!

All I wanted

All I ever wanted, was
someone who can
a true friend!

Someone that will look
into my eyes,
and see how much I'm
hurting, without
me telling them!

Someone that will just
give me a
warm, loving hug
without even asking!

That friend that can
just look at my
smile and tell
the secrets it holds!

All I ever wanted was
a friend who
could make me laugh
through my tears!

A friend that can just
      hear the sadness in
  my voice and see
        my pain in my
text!

All I wanted was a
        friend who was small
   on words, but
      big on actions!

એ ઈ' એ

Alone

I'm all alone,
I was abandoned by
the people I thought
were my friends.

I feel like my life
has faded away
into the darkness.

My heart has been
played around with like a
basketball!

My soul is drifting in
the wind,
with nowhere to go.

My tears have become
a waterfall, of
sadness.

My anger has driven
me crazy,
to the point, that I
can't think!

This is me now, because,
I am all,
Alone.

☙ ℬ ☙

Amusing

They is one thing I love
    seeing in life!

It's funny how people believe
    they know you!

To make it funnier, how they believe
    they own your life!

Just to make it hilarious when they
    believe you are happy!

I find it very amusing when
    you think I'm stupid!

I just wish people knew that they
    are wrong on how they
  see me!

Cause if they knew my life
    they would understand why
I do certain things!

భ ద భ

Appreciation

Be thankful some people are
forgiving!
Be thankful they don't
hold grudges!

Be grateful you have
a family!
Be grateful you are
loved!

Appreciate what you
have!
Appreciate that you
are alive!

Why can't you be pleased!

Have gratitude you
still have
Parents!

ᚠ ᚠ ᚠ

Awesome Five

To my friend who's a
        savage but
    always has my back when I need
            her!
Thank you, you taught me what
        a friend is!

My twin who always
        says crazy things
    but at the same time, he gives the
            best advise!
Thank you I leant much
                More than I thought
        I knew!

To my Boo who always helps
        me and does stupid
    things with me!
Thank you I learnt too always
        stay true to myself!

To my Sir who I think
            is missing some
    sense, but has many jokes!
        Thank you, you taught me hard times don't last!

To my Butterscotch who's
just a crazy
girlfriend who speaks her mind!
Thank you, you taught me my
Happiness comes first!

In them found a friend
that I can
always depend on either on
sunny bright days or even
on rainy cold days!
They are the true definition
of real friends!

Back

Depression is Back!
I guess it never left
Watching me everyday
Picking up the pieces of my life
Laughing at me through the cracks

Loneliness is Back!
Maybe it never left
waiting patiently for everyone to leave
searching for all my insecurities

The Memories are Back!
Flooding my brain with all the darkness
flushing my past like lightening
smiling at how it has gotten me back!

Darkness is Back!
I guess he will never leave
keeping me company when I was kicked out the light
Insuring me he will always stay with me!

Anxiety is Back!
she feeds on my happiness
she turns my happiness into sadness
she has installed fear in me!

Be yourself

Why *do* we live our?
   lives in fear!

Fear of what people think
   or see you!

Why should we compare our-
      selves with
   others!

Why *do* we live our lives?
      making other's
   happy instead of ourselves!

Why can't we make ourselves?
      happy but can
   make other's happy!

Does it really matter if?
      people like you
   or don't!

Why can't you just be
      yourself, then
   pretending to be something
      you're not!

B B B

Beautiful

Nine words that describe
a beautiful person!

B – for Bold you are venturous,
dashing and self-assured.

E – for Elegant you are majestic,
imposing and solemn.

A – for Astonishing you make the men
jaw-drop, you stun the world with
your beauty.

U – for Unique you stand out like a
Blue Moon in the clear dark sky, you are universal
like Venus between the stars.

T – for Tender-hearted you are devoted, fond,
compassionate and affectionate.

I – for Intelligent, you are ultrasmart
which makes you stand out from the crowd.

F – for Flower, you are dazzling you are like a
pearl from the ocean your warm heart blossoms the world.

U – for Uplifting you are hope, encouragement you are
beyond extreme you are more than what you are
inside than on the outside.

L – for Loving you show love to everyone you
care about you put others feelings
before yours.

That's what makes you beautiful!

Beloved

Thank you for our smile!
Thank you for your generosity!
Thank you for all those happy days!
 I'll dearly miss all this
  things!

Your personality went with your
  name "beloved"!

Death has taken your beautiful
 soul!
And left us in sorrow!

Death has left us in grief,
 it has taken away
a soul that was pure!

Death covered him with his
 wing and left with
him!

But, death never took our
 memories of you!
Will forever cherish you!
 We love you beloved!

Biggest Regret

My biggest regret
　　was you,
I regret everything
　　about you!

I regret the day
　　I met you!

I regret the day
　　we became friends!
I regret the day
　　I began to
develop feelings for
　　you!

I regret the day
　　I opened up
　　　to you!

I regret the day
　　we started
　　　dating!

You were the biggest mistake
　　in my life!

Broken

I'm hurt not just
      on the outside
but also, on the
    inside!

I'm broken not just
    my heart
but beyond my
   soul!

I'm torn from every
    inch of
my body!

I feel like my soul
    has been
  ripped from my
    body!

My body is lifeless like
    a protea that
receives no water!

I am broken from my surface to
    my core!

Broken down

I trusted him so
    much I felt
safe when I was near
    him!
I cherished him unconditionally
    to the point I
got addicted to his tenderness!

I thought he cared for me like
    a sister!
  Also, as his own child!

    But it was all a lie!

He made me part of them,
    he took away
  my purity, my innocence!

He turned me into a
    victim!

That one thing that mattered
    was ripped out of
me!

Daily Questions?

What happened to
    me?

Where has all my love,
      tenderness
   and joy, gone too?

What has become of
     me?
  How did I get here?

Who was the cause of?
    my endless
      sadness!

When did I change to?
    become what
I have become?

Why did it happen to?
   me, why
must I suffer?

What did I do to deserve?
    this life.

Darkness

When everyone turned
    they back on
me, Darkness
       kept me company!

When my friends hanged
    out together and
I was not invited
     Darkness would
say don't worry, you
    don't fit in anyways!

When I was bullied
    and pushed around by
people I loved,
    Darkness would say just
use the razor it will release
      the pain!

When I would cry and
     wished to die
Darkness would say
     Just commit suicide!

Darkness stuck with me
    through my good and
bad times!

Death 1

One may have felt
　　　this pain
or maybe not!

That one pain
　　　that doesn't
fade but only
　　　grows!

It's an endless
　　　torment
that excruciate you
　　　forever!

It haunts you day in
　　　and day out!

One may understand what
　　　I'm talking
　　about,
One may, just think I'm
　　　crazy!

One day you'll understand
　　　when it happens
but for now, just enjoy life!

Death 2

Death a simple word
      with a simple
            definition!

A word that looks harmless
         but has a horrible
   truth!

It's described as cold, dark,
         scary and a nightmare!

Such a simple word but
         has a terrifying
   origin!

Death a word that sounds like
         depth but is not
      what is meant!

Death the opposite of life
      and has a painful
            truth!

Death it haunts you until
         he gets a
            grep of his
prey!

Death 3

He creeps in the cracks
  of the windy nights,
He hides behind shadows
  ready to attack!

He havours around
  the weak
and devours on fear!

He moves like wind and
  strikes like lightening!

Beware he's always watching
  waiting for midnight to
strike
  to get his next victim!

He's everyone's fear and nightmare
  But no matter how much
you run and hide,
  he will always catch up and find
you!

We call him heartless but he's real name is
  Death!

Deep Down

How well do you know?
 your friend!
Do you know her on the outside?
 or, do you
 know her even
 deeper!
Can you tell the difference?
 from her real
 smile and fake smile!

Can you look into her
 eyes and tell
 that they are full of sadness!

Can you look at her actions
 and see that
 her spirit is down!

When she spends time
 alone and shuts everyone
out,
 do you start asking yourself, why?

When she starts wearing
              long sleeves, and
long trousers,
       do you wonder what
     has happened to her skin!

Can you hear the
       pain in her voice
     over the phone
              or
     can't you!
How deep do you know
       Your friend!

❧ ℬ ❧

Deeper

I am falling deeper
into the
darkness!

I have fallen deeper
into my own
nightmare!

I have cut myself deeper
then a pit!

I have lost my life in
the darkness!

I have traded my life to
the demons!
They have taken my light
and have replaced
it with the
darkness!
That is how much I
have fallen
deeper!

Depression

Depression is not just being
sad,
No, but feeling an unknown pain in
your heart.

It is a never ending
pain in your heart
you live with
soreness forever!

Depression takes away your
happiness,
And leaves you with scars
that will never
Heal!

You feel like you
don't belong
anywhere!
You don't control Depression
instead
it controls you!

Describe Me

Describe me!

They are words people
love to describe
me with, like:
Fat, ugly, stupid and unattractive

They even have things to
tease me about like
my weight, height, behaviour
and personality

But that's how they me!

I describe myself as
Palm instead of fat, Beautiful instead of ugly,
Smart instead of stupid and Appealing instead of unattractive!

So how would you describe me?

Different

I am unique cause I am
Different,
I am special in my own
way!

I don't follow the trend
I create my own
trend!

I am creative, I'm unique
I am not, like other girls!
I am different in
my way!

I may not be the smartest but,
at least I know
how to love!

I may not be the prettiest but,
at least I know
how to care for
others!

That's what makes
me different!

Disappear

I wonder how it feels like to
        have real friends!

I wonder what it's like to
        be genuinely happy!

I wonder how it feels like
        to have a purpose in
life!

I wish I knew what's it
        like to have a meaning
life!

I wonder what it's like to
        be loved for who you are,
not what you have!

I wonder what's it like to
        feel physical pain!

I wish all this depression
        could disappear!

Do Not

Why do you care about
      what people say?
Does it really
         matter?

Why does it affect
      you?
  Why do you let
    them
    Bring you down?

Why should you care?

Do you really have to
    hurt yourself
       over people who
don't care?

What do you benefit from
    listening to them?

Do not let people bringing
          you down over
mere words!

What they say should not
      matter cause it's
          your life alone!

Do you!

Do you still love me?
or don't you,
cause right now I feel, like
you don't.

Do you cherish me like, you
used too?
Do you still consider me,
your friend?

Do you, or don't you?
just be honest with
me!

Do you enjoy seeing me
        hurt and
            heartbroken?

Do you love seeing me
        depressed and
                hopeless?

Don't think I'm stupid I
        can see everything!

Do You

Do you know why
       I don't cry anymore, it's
   because I spent
            years, months, weeks, days, hours,
                 minutes and seconds
         crying my eye-bowls out!

Do you know why I don't
           tell anyone how
   I really feel?
        it's because of judgement!

Do you know why I don't
        care about how,
   I look?
       because my confidence and self-love
was ripped out!

Do you know what it feels
        like to be me?
   to wake-up and wish you could have
         stayed asleep!

Do you know why I am
        still alive?
    It's because of oxygen!

Do you know why I love
        sleeping? it's
    because I don't feel
        anything!

Do you know why I
            know the truth of life?
        that's because of the pain
                    that life bought for me!

Do you?

Do you really love me?
Do you love me for me?
and not my
things!

Do you treasure my heart?
like I treasure
yours!

Do you miss me when
you are alone?
Do you still love me the
same?

I am scared of where our
love is going!
But I hope it will succeed
at the end!

Cause it feels like I am losing
you very, slowly!

Don't be deceived

Don't be fooled,
I've
been there!

Don't listen to
them!
At the end you'll
look like a
fool!

Don't trust anyone
trust yourself!
That was my biggest
mistake!

Don't ignore your
past!
It will haunt
you!

Don't run away from your
emotions!
They'll catch up to
you one day!

Don't be deceived!
        Listen to yourself
Trust no one but your
        heart!

Emotions

My emotions stream down
my face like a waterfall!
I want to love but,
I can't!

I want to smile and show my white teeth, but I
don't know how too!

I want to be happy, excited over the moon, but I
can't!

I want to cry like others, but
my eyes are too dry!

Why am I emotionless?

Enough

Do you ever ask yourself?
   why I never
      cut too deep?

I only cut deep enough to feel
      the pain and see the blood
         but, not
      deep enough to kill myself!

      Because

I don't want to hurt you,
      but, the
   reason I hurt myself is because
      of you!

The reason I'm tired is,
      because,
         of all the pain you
   have coursed me!

Ever

When you think you
   have it
all, but
      actually you
   don't!

When you thought you
      were loved
   but honestly
         you weren't!

When you listened to your
      brain instead
   of your instinct!

When you think
      someone cared about you
but actually
   nobody cared!

When you think life
      was easy
   but then it showed you
      it's not!

Everyday

Every day, every night its
    the same process all over
  again!

All those memories come
        dancing around,
    the voices come
            singing!

The craving gets stronger
        each time, and
    the stronger they get
            the deeper I go!

The pain builds up and
        numbs the
            memories!

The need of being
        helped creeps along,
    but, disappears
            when judgement enters!

All the emotions start
        mixing together,
trying to create a tornado!

The eyes start stinking
        and becoming
    blur from the
            tears!

And, every time I just
        pray and wish I could
stay asleep and
            not wake up the next day!
Then I will know the process
            has come to an end!

Faded

I'm fading, only this
    time, they
no coming out!

I can see the light
    slowly becoming
dime!

As the light becomes
    dime,
    darkness is slowly filling
        up the space!

What I once saw as colourful
    and breath-taking
  I now see as dark as coal
    and gruesome!

Those red roses that once
    attracted my attention, now
  blind my sight by
      the brightness!

This time around
      I don't see myself
  Coming out!

This time I don't
      think the light will
  be able to reach
      me!

This time around
      I've fallen into
  it too deep!

To the point the
      light has faded away
That the only thing
       that remains is the
  darkness!

Failure

I'm a failure, I have
failed everyone in
        my life!

I failed as a daughter!
I failed as a friend!
I failed as a sister!
I failed as a girlfriend!
I failed as a niece!
I failed as an auntie!
I failed as a granddaughter!

I'm a failure, and I will
always be a
        failure!

Everyone had faith in me
        but,
    I just let them all
        down!

I was born into failure and
        I will die as a
            failure!

※ ℬ ※

Fake love

You love a person so much
that you would do
anything for them!
You love them so
Unconditionally!

But the love for you,
is fake!

You love a person that
your love for them
is unlimited!
You love them so deeply,
That it drives you
insane!

But they love is
fake!

You love the person so much
that you can't
stop thinking of them day, and
night!

But they don't feel
the same for you!

℔ ℏ ℔

Father's Love

I wish people could
        stop lying!
I wish they could just
     be honest!

It's not true when they
       say a mother's
   Love is stronger!

A mother's love is
      stronger but
  A Father's love is the
strongest!

A Father's love can not
     be pierced
   even by a diamond!

It never fades, it just
    grows deeper
no matter the distance!

Wait I think, I got it
    mixed up, a mother's
love is the strongest!

No, wait, to you
but for
me a father's love is
the strongest!

℣ ℞ ℣

Fear

I don't fear people,
or death,

But I fear life,
cause its hard
and stressful

I fear not
being loved,

I fear losing
the people
I love and
care about!

Life can be hard,
but it is
Precious to live,

Don't fear life
like me!

Feelings

Don't judge what you do
        not know!

Cause you don't know how
        it feels like to be
    me!

You don't know how much
        pain I have gone
    through!

You don't know what it's like
    to be made a fool of everyday
of your life!

You have never tried to commit
        suicide cause everyone in your
    life doesn't care about
                you!

Have you ever taken a razor?
        and sliced your wrist like
slicing meat!

So, don't judge me before you have
        felt my pain!

Fine

The word "Fine" may
look, plain
and dull!

But it hides a
lot of secrets!

Do you ever ask yourself?
why people like me
just say "I'm Fine"!

That's because it describes
all the emotions we are
feeling!

"Fine", is not just "fine",
"fine", is depressed, heartbroken,
anxious, sad, hopeless, worthless
or worse
emotionless!

"Fine" is not "fine" it's
just a nicer way
to hide your true feelings from
the world!

Fire in my soul

The fire in my soul
burns like a
burning forest!

The fire in my soul
gives me strength
and power!

My fire in my soul
gives me courage
like a warrior!

My fire will always live
in me until
I die!

That fire in my soul has
created my
personality!

Friends are Fake

I was told never
beg a person to be
your friend

People you once thought were
your friends were actually
fake and not real

Friends come and go,
When you need them
they are never there
for you

So, let me tell you something
don't for a friend who left
you!

Foundation and Walls

The hardest thing I have
        ever done was trusting
                people too much,
To trust them to the point
        I become blinded and
                fooled at the same time!

        But trust can be
                built again!

The saddest part is that
        Trusting and being honesty
Again!
No matter how much you try to
        be honest about how you
feel,
        you will see you can never be
honest again with a person that broke your trust
                instead, your trust
        will be built on lies!

        Trust can be built either on honesty
                or on lies!

Honesty is the foundation and Trust
        is the walls,
If honesty doesn't exist trust will
            collapse once again!

Gentle

So calm, so gentle, so peaceful!
Like the ocean bed,
in summer!

So fragile, so delicate, so precious!
Like a priceless
vase!

So strong, so brave, so fearless!
Like a soldier in
war!

Your heart is as bold as a
cub!
You are blessed you are
you!

Good and Bad Times

They say every month is
         special in a different
    unique way!

Well for me every month hold's
         the saddest moment's
    in my life!

January is a month of
         new beginnings
    but for me it's the time
         were it took away my
Mother!

February is a month of
         love and friendship
    for me it's the month of
              sorrow and grief for
my friend!

March is the month of Human Right's
         well not for
me, that was the month were
         were my depression
started!

April is a month of Easter and
        family in my
  case it's the month my heart
            was broken!

May has nothing special
        but symbolizes success and love,
            funny thing I'm not love
instead, I'm hatred!

June the month of Youth
            it's the month were
I made a big mistake!

July is the month of passion
        and love, This
is the month I wished I
            had my mother!

August is the month of women
        and vacation,
    for me it's a month of
                loss and memories!

September is the month of spring
            to blossom,
    with flowers that have a drop
                of innocent blood!
October the month of stunning
            beauty,
    the month I lost my friend,
                my sister to betrayal!

November the month of preparations
            for the holidays and fun,
    it's a month I lost love and trust
        for everyone!

December is the month of festivity
not for little me,
it's the month I became an orphan!

Every month has it's good and bad
events!

Good Days

What happened to the
Good Days?
When we would laugh,
and smile
together?

We would crack jokes together,
laugh together,
We would go crazy out of
control!

Now you have changed you
don't laugh and
smile these days!

You are always moody,
you don't
Talk to me anymore.

I miss the good old
days,
I hope you miss
them too!

Happily

I can't wait for the day
    I lose all hope!

The day I take my last breath,
      and my last beat!
The day when my body becomes cold
        like a cooler!

When that day comes, I hope you
      will be happy!

When that day comes, my suffering will
        be over, my pain, my emotions,
           my depression, my anxiety but
    most of all my life,
        will be over!

When that day comes, I will truly
      be happy and I will
          happily, go to sleep!

Happiness 1

Was it worth it?
    Yes!
Was it needed?
    Yes!

Will you ever want
    to stop?
Will you ever
    consider getting help!

Don't you feel
    pain?
Don't you want to
    heal?

Were, your cuts
    worth it!
Was it worth?
    destroying all
your beauty!

    For others
happiness!

Happiness 2

Your happiness makes me
smile,
Happiness is what makes me
sing and dance,
Happiness is what makes
my heart beat
faster!

Happiness brings peace in
my heart,
Your happiness is everything
in me!

Happiness is what gives me
strength,
To laugh, have fun and to
go on adventures!

Happiness is everything
to me!

Hate

Why *do* I have so
much hate?
Why was it invested
in my heart?

Why *does* my hate
get the best
of me?

Why is it the
Strongest
emotion in me?

Why *does* it take
away,
My joy and happiness?

My hate takes away
My love and
replaces it with,
so much anger!

$\mathcal{D} \ \mathcal{B} \ \mathcal{D}$

Heart and Mind

My heart is at war
        while my mind
is relaxing!

My heart is battling with
        My emotions
while my mind is thinking about
        Tomorrow!

My heart is locking itself up
        to let no one in,
While my mind is open for
        Anyone!

My heart is insecure about
        itself and builds up walls
While my mind doesn't even have
        Any!

My heart and mind work opposite
        each other that's why
            They're always battling!

Her Trust

She trusted you with her
life,
But you betrayed her!

Now she screams from the
ground,
Her blood is dripping from your
hands!

She trusted you like her own
brother,
But you used her trust against
her!

Her trust was the size of the
Nile River!

But you stabbed her on
her back!

Hurt Me

I only have one question
in my life!

Why is it okay for you to hurt
me, but
I can't myself?

It's okay for you to break me
apart,
but I can't cut myself!

It's okay for you to use me
but I can't use a
razor!

So, it's okay if you make my life
a living hell
but I'm not allowed to
go to hell!

It's okey for you to laugh at
me, but
I'm not allowed to cry!
Why can you hurt me
but I can't hurt myself?

Hurt you

Why do you let them
      hurt you?

Yes! They may be prettier,
      smarter and better than
         You!

    But!

You are also unique in
      your own special
  way!

You may be ugly but
      some people don't
care!

Why should you care
      about they
  opinions!

What they say isn't
      important, it's how
  you see yourself
      that's important!

How I feel

I'm cold like
ice,
Every breath I take feels
like I'm being
stung by bees!

My heart feels like I've
been stabbed with multiple
knives at once!

My body is numb as
if I have been run
over by a
truck!

My thoughts are suicidal,
my dreams are
bloody!

My eyes are red and
baggy,
from the tears!

My weight has become
less from starvation!

How Much

It's sad when you think,
  you know me!
      But, actually
  you don't!

It's sad when you say, you
  love me!
      But, you
  don't know the definition!

It's sad when you consider
  me a friend!
      But, I
  don't!

It's sad when you think
  I care!
      But, darling
  I don't even bother!

Every time I say I love
  you!
Do you ever ask yourself?
      does she
  really mean it!

I!

I love the way you,
love me, but
it feels like I don't
love you!

I feel like you are
fading away,
from me day after day!

I still love you very,
much but my,
mind is starting to
control my,
Heart!

❧ ❧ ❧

I am Sorry

I'm sorry, I'm sorry!
   I'm sorry for
   everything!

I'm sorry I was
   born,
I'm sorry, I'm not
   perfect!

I'm sorry, I'm always
   depressed,
I'm sorry, I always
   cut myself!

I'm sorry, I'm in your
   life,
I'm sorry, for all the
   pain I've coursed
   you!

But most of
All!

I'm sorry, I didn't stop
   loving you!

I can't

I can't do this
anymore!
I am tired of this
life!

I can't take this
pain anymore!

I am sick and tired
of the pain
in me!

I can't take this
anxiety anymore!

I am tired of seeing
my blood dripping
and the
scars on my
wrists!

I don't want to live
this life anymore!
I want to rest so the
pain can go away!

I don't

I don't love you the
way I did
back then!

I don't feel the chemistry
that we had
before!

My love for you has been
replaced by someone
else!

He has taken my love from
you and now
belongs to him!

I don't want to do this but
I don't love you
anymore!

I don't like to see you
hurt like this!
I don't want you cry for me
but to find happiness
like me!

I love you

I love you!
I love you more than
Anyone I have ever
loved!

I love the way you care for
the people around
you!

I love the way you care
for nature and
how you treat
it!

I love how you put me
first in your
life,
Then anyone else!

I will always love you!

I miss you

I think of you day and
night,
I cannot stop thinking about
you!

Your name is all over my
mind,
Thinking about you makes me
want to burst into
tears!

I look at my reflection and
I see your reflection behind me
But,
when I turn to see if it's you
you're not there!

Why does it hurt when I
miss you?
But doesn't when I am with
you

I miss you!
Do you miss me!

Inner Beauty

Your inner beauty is not
how you
look!

Your inner beauty is inside
your heart!

It is how you treat people,
around you!

You are more gorgeous on
the inside than on
the outside!

Your inner beauty shines like
a diamond!

Your inner beauty is as beautiful
as the raising
sun!

Your heart brings happiness to
people around
you!

It's about you only

In life it's not
    about others!
It's about you,
    and you
  alone!

It's not about impressing
        other people!
It's not about how they
    see you!

In life it's about how
    you see yourself!
It's about impressing
        yourself and yourself
  alone!

To live a life impressing
    others is like
living a life that's not
    even yours!

Why do I need to care
    about other's opinion
        when it doesn't even matter!

ℰ ℬ ℰ

It hurt's

It hurt's so much!
You have hurt me so
much I have
forgotten who I am
in life!

You have hurt me physically,
Emotionally and Mentally!

You have destroyed my self-
esteem!
You have taken away my
smile!

You have hurt me more
then a bullet!

You have hurt me so much
that the pain sails in
my mind
24/7!

That is how much it
hurts!

ꗃ ꗃ ꗃ

It Hurt's

It hurt's to see you
frown,
without a smile on your
cute face!

I miss your laughter,
and jokes!
It kills me to see you
this down!

I wish I could bring back,
your happiness!
And laughter and your beautiful
smile!

Judging

Why does everyone have to
judge one
another!

Why are we so quick to
judge a person
because of they,
appearance, weights, beliefs and
skin colour!

They is a say: "Don't judge
a book by it's
cover!

But, why is it that we are
always judging
people,
Before we have known
them better!

Why can't we learn to?
love one another
as family!
Then always judging each
other!

Learning

I am learning to love
      my imperfections,
  to accept my fallible!

It may not be easy
      but
   I will learn!

I am learning to live
    in the darkness, cause
I am able to see the sparkling stars!

I am learning to accept
     that I'm a loner
   cause, I am able to have to clear
      mind!

I am learning to love my
     scars cause they,
show how many battles I have
      won!

I have learnt that nobody
     will ever understand me!
But it doesn't matter!

❧ ✿ ❧

Left for

Let me give you
   four reasons why
she died!

She was tired of pain,
    the pain destroyed
her life!

She had enough of
     judgement, it
destroyed her self-esteem!

She was useless as a
   human and had no
reason to live
    because the people
she loved all left her!

Her purity was taken away
    by someone she
thought would protect her!

She killed herself because
    she had
nothing left to live for!

Let Him Go

If I had to die
   today!
I wonder how things
      would be!

Would things stay the
      same,
   or change for the best or
worst!

If I had to die
   today!
Will people cry for me?
         or
   celebrate!

If I had to die
   today!
Will I still be remembered?
      or will I be forgotten!

If death had to take
      me!
will you follow him or
   let him go!

Life

Life is hard and takes away
your strength,
Life makes you want to give up,
on everything!

Life is a roller coaster ride!
It destroys everything in
It's path!

Life takes away your happiness
and leaves you with
sadness,

Life takes away everything you loved,
And leaves you,
in grief!

Life eats your soul very
slowly,
Life is a curse and not
a blessing!

But life will always
be life!

Life Test

I was tested
    again!
And I failed the
    test!

I avoided my past
    and
        now I regret doing so!

My depression was knocking
    and I let it in
        that was a bad decision!

I bought the devil inside
    and now his torturing
        me like hell!

I don't regret letting him
    in but I
    regret letting him leave
        in the first place!

I don't regret my past
    but I'm
        proud of it!

Lonely

It's cold and dark
my heart beats for
me!

I'm lonely not because
I wanted
I'm lonely because of
love and trust

I'm lonely from yesterday
from today and from
tomorrow!

I will remain lonely to the
day I perish!

ॐ ॐ' ॐ

Love

What is the meaning
of love?

Love is not just a word
but an action
from deep inside your
Heart!

When you truly love
someone,
You show them by your
actions!

You don't love a person
for they looks or things
But for,
They heart and kindness!

You put them first in your
life,
Then anything or anyone
else!

That is what love means!

Loved

I will be honest with
            you!
I have more weapons than
            enemies!

I have more black clothes
            than any other colours!

I have more sweaters than
            shoes!

I've lost more blood than
            I drink water!

I've died more than I've
            lived!

I have cried more than I've
            laughed!

I've been hated more than I've
            been loved!

Love Dies

Enjoy it will it lasts,
cause once its gone its gone!
Cherish I will you still
can cause once it's gone
you can never get it
back!

It fades away like a memory
from the past,
It wilts like a flower that
has no water.

Love runs out like a tape
with no water!
It flows out of your heart
like a stream flowing down a
waterfall!

Enjoy will you can cause
once it dies
It's gone!

Love Hurt's

Why!

Why does it hurt,
Do you feel the
pain that
I feel inside!

Why does love have
to hurt so
much!

Why does it pierce,
through my heart
like a bullet!

My heart runs
faster then
a,
cheetah!

Love may hurt!
But,
My love for him is real!

Me to her

Don't compare me
to her!

She's herself and I'm
myself!

She has an hourglass body and
I don't!

She is popular and loved
and me well I'm
hated!

Her body attracts every
boy and mine just makes
them run, the opposite
direction!

She's perfect and I'm
not!

So, don't compare me to
her!

Meant!

Is it you or is it me,
I don't know what to,
do anymore!

Was I wrong or were you,
wrong!
Am I the problem or is it
you!

I can't do this anymore,
maybe it wasn't
meant to be!

But just know that I love,
you!

Melted

My heart was as
    strong as,
  Diamond!

My heart was cold and
    tuff like iron and
        steel!

That all changed when he
    come along!

He melted my heart and it
    become pure
  like glass!

It became fragile and
    delicate like
a glass crystal!

My heart become soft like
    a pool full of
  feathers!

He taught me love,
    that can be cherished!

Mistake in Life

I was a mistake to
        be born!
The day I learnt to
        walk was a
mistake!

All the love I received
        was all a
            mistake!

The day people cared about
            my emotions, was
        a mistake!

The day when I began
        to love and
        cherish was a mistake!

When I began to show
        kindness to people
    it was a mistake!

My whole life has always
        been a mistake
    and will forever be a mistake!

Mommy

I love you!

You are my world, my happiness
you're all I
need in my
life!

It's you who makes me
want to wake
up!

You are the person I live
for!
Your all I think of,
it's you who gives
me strength!

You're my piler of balance
you are my sunshine
when I am blue!

You are one of a kind
you are rare
like a black pearl!
You make me sparkle like
an Opal gem!

Months of the Year

January the month of
poverty, the month of
starvation!

February the month of
love, the month of
happiness!

March the month of
freedom, the month of
rights!

April the month of
easter, the month of
peace!

May the month of
queens, our dearest
mothers!

June the month of
struggles, to cherish the
student that died.

July the month of
Nelson, the father of
the nation!

August the month of
women, the rocks of
the nations!

September the month
heritage, to share our
culture!

October the month of
horror, the month of my
ghost friends!

November the month of
it's almost over, to
prepare yourself!

December the month of
family, the month of
celebration!

Move-On

When will I start?
doing something
I love and enjoy!

When will I stop?
satisfying other's rather
than myself!

When will the day come?
were I make myself happy?
instead of making others
happy!

When will I stop listening?
to people's opinion about
me, rather than listening
to my own!

Why do I keep satisfying people?
with my tears and blood!

Why can't I learn to leave?
them and move-on!

My

My life is like a roller-coaster
ride,
My heart is made from
stone!

My demons' control who
I am,
My eyes are like the eyes
of a wolf!

My strength is like the
strength of a lion,
My roar is like the roar
of a tiger!

My sight is like the
sight of an owl,
My speed is like the
speed of a cheetah!

I am not just an
ordinary girl,
But a girl who is
combined with,
Powerful animals!

My Anger

My anger is so much
that I can not
control it!

My anger turns me into
a vicious animal!

It controls my mind like
a puppet!

My anger takes over my
body like I'm possessed
with a demon!

My anger has turned my
heart from red
to black!

My beloved ones

It's true what they
say!
It's no lie when
they say it!

They never hated
me!
It was me who hated
them!

They wanted to bond
with me!
But I never gave them
the time!

They couldn't reach out
to me!
They tried to warn me!

They stopped trying, but they
never stopped
loving me!
They stopped warning me, but
still cared for
me!

They always protected
me!
They always watched
me!

They love me too the
day they
died!

But

My beloved Parents will always
be in my
heart!

My best

I know, I was wrong!
I tried, but
you pushed me
away!

I promised you but, I
couldn't do it anymore!

I pushed myself
But,
you just pushed me away!

You don't look at me
like before!

I tried my best!

$\mathcal{D}$ $\mathcal{B}$ $\mathcal{D}$

My best friend

My best friend may not be
the best looking,
But I love him the way
he is!

He may not be smart
but,
He cares for me and respects
me!

He may be annoying
but,
He doesn't pretend to be
something he is not!
My best friend is my piler of
life,
He is my soul and spirit
of joy!

My Coldness

I am so cold like a
deep freezer,
My heart is cold like
ice!

My emotions are cold like
ice cubes!
My fingers are frozen like
snow!

My coldness has taken over
my whole
body!

My coldness has frozen my
heart!
My coldness has frozen my
soul and spirit!

My Cut

My first cut was
for being
alive!

My second cut is
for falling in
love!

My third cut is
for my
past!

My fourth cut is
for this
stupid depression!

My fifth cut is
for caring
about life!

My sixth cut is
for the people
who love me!

Just one more cut!

My Death

Am I dead or alive?
Who am I, what am I?
What is my purpose for
living?

Am I a girl or a boy?
Why was I born?
Who created me?

Why am I so cold as ice?
Why am I numb?
Why is it dark around
me?

I'm not alive, I am,
dead!
Death swift me by
my feet!

My death was a
mystery,
And will remain a
mystery!

My first kiss

My first kiss was on
top of the
hill!
When the moon was
shining very
bright onto
us!

He leaned close to my
lips!
His eyes shone brighter
than the constant
stars above!

His lips were softer than
the palm of a
baby!

My heart melt and my
guard was let
down by his
love!

He stole my kiss and
my heart like a Jewel thief!

My heart

My heart is bleeding out
for you!
My love for you is so
much, I can not
control it!

But you do not bleed your
heart out for me!
You do not show me that you
love me!

Do you still love me like you,
did before!
You don't treat me the same
anymore!

My Journey

My life is full of sadness
and tears!
I have had a bad
past!
My journey in life has been
miserable,
I have struggled to be who
I am!

My journey may have been
difficult but,
I have survived!

Look at me now!

My life

I was born a mess!
Now,
My life has become a
mess!

My life is full of
sadness,
My life is a curse
and will always
be a curse!

My life is like a
road,
That has potholes,
and cracks!

My life is not a walk in
the park,
But,
My life is like a heartbeat
that has ups and
downs!

❦ ❦ ❦

My love for you

My love for you is so
much that I can't
count it,
My love for you is the
size of the
ocean!

I have never felt this
way for any
body!

My heart beats fast when
I look into your
eyes!

I love you like I have
never loved
before.

My Memories

My memories about my
past,
Is a never ending
nightmare!

My memories make me sweat
like a dog,
My memories haunt me too
this very day!

My memories are not the
best ones,
My memories are dark and
are cold like
the coldest day
of winter!

My memories drive me
insane!
My memories control my
mind!

My memories will always
haunt me to
the day I
die!

118

My Pain 1

Don't feel for me
when I'm hurt!

Don't be sorry when you
break me!

Don't regret it when you
made me self-esteem low!

Don't help me when I
cut myself!

Don't tell anyone I'm
depressed!

Don't cry when I am
dead!

Don't act like you care
when you didn't!

Don't visit my grave to
apologize when you are
the reason I'm there!

My Pain 2

You think I'm happy,
      well, I'm not!

I just don't want to
      show the pain
  you have bought in my life!

You think I'm strong,
      Well guess what I'm broken!

I just don't want you
      to see how broken
I am!

You think I have a
      perfect life!

If only you knew how
      much times, a cry
when I'm alone!

You think I want attention,
      if only you knew!

All I want is someone
      to help me and understand
  my pain!

శ B శ

My Scars

My scars are my memory of
the past,
When I see them, I think of
what caused
them!
My scars are deeper than a pit
I wear long sleeves to
cover them from people
around me!

My scars are the most effective
thing to me!
My cuts are painless but my
heart is full of sorrow!

I have over a hundred scars
that I created,
Not because I wanted too, no
But because of the pain.

It pierces through the heart and
leaves a big hole!
My scars are memories that I
Will never forget.

My shame

I loved myself, so
     much that the
mirror was my
     best friend!
      But,
That all changed slowly!

Every time someone told me
     I was ugly
or insulted my body!

I slowly lost interest in
     my best friend
 not only that,
     I started hating my
  body!

The more I got insulted
   the more I started
to despite my body!

   Peoples words tore my
    heart and
     soul!

My tears

My tears fill up the
dams,
My tears run down my
face like a
waterfall!

My tears are not the
tears of joy,
but,
the tears of sadness!

My tears make me
Stronger,
They create my
personality!

My tears feel like
acid,
But they create who I
am meant to
be in life!

My thoughts

My heart is racing faster,
than an anaconda!

My mind is racing with my
thoughts!

My thoughts are driving me
insane to the point, that
I need a break.

I can't anymore, this
is driving me
bananas.

My true love

You were my
   life, my joy!

You made me
   smile when
I was upside down!
   but now you're
      gone!

You've left me alone
      in this cruel
world!

You left with all
   the love
I had in me!

You left me when I
      didn't expect
it!

You cherished me, and
loved me
unconditionally!

But,
Faith, will bring you
back to me!

My World

My imaginary world!
Water slides, diamond
rivers, gold trees with crystals!

Unicorns in the sky,
mermaids by the rocks
singing!

Floating castles, flying dishes,
talking pots.

Flying tigers, jumping snakes,
dancing elephants!

Gold skies, silver moon, pink
water, purple grass!

What more does my perfect
world need!

Myself

Some say I'm fat
　　　While I say I'm
Plump!

Some call me stupid
　　　While I call myself
Intelligent!

Some think I'm boring
　　　While I think I'm
Bubbly!

Some say I'm annoying
　　　While I say I'm
Just being Me!

Some call me plain
　　　While I call myself
Rare!

They think about me
　　　But,
　　I think of myself!

Nightmare

Roses are red like
        my blood!

Knives are sharp like
        my razor!

Graves are deep as
        my wounds!

Depression is like being
        Mentally disabled!

Water remembers the past
        like I remember everything
that has happened!

I am loosely like the moon
        that shines at
                night!

I am negative about life
        and I never think of
positive things!

Remember me because I'll be back!

Nobody

Nobody knows what I feel
    or how it feels to be me!

To have no purpose to
    wake-up in the morning!

To be told everyday how worthless
    you are in life!

To push people away cause you're
    scared of being hurt!

To always wear long clothes, just to
    hide your scars!

To constantly here voices in your
    head!

To continuously feel like you don't
    belong anywhere!

    But

Nobody knows how it's like
    to have a razor as a friend!

Not Friends

I call her my "friend"
      and she calls
me her friend!

We laugh and show love
      for one another!

      But let me tell
            you a secret!

I don't love or care about
            her!

I pretend to love her that's
      why she's my "friend"!

I want to tell her I'm not
      her friend!

I want her to stop laughing with
      me cause I'm not her
            friend!

      But, her
"frenemy"!

Old Me

Nobody knows what I miss
     the most in life!

I miss the old me, the
     real me!

I miss my gorgeous smile
     showing my perfect teeth!

I miss wearing open clothes,
     showing my flawless skin!

I miss not caring what people said
     because I knew I was worth it!

I miss being happy and well
     cause I was alive!

I miss waking up in the morning
     knowing I have a purpose
to live!

Now I don't even know who I really
     am!
I miss the old me!

ॐ ఔ ॐ

Pain

Do you enjoy seeing
        me hurt,
                in tears, with pain!

Do you find it funny when
        I'm depressed
                cause of the pain!

Why do you hurt me so much?
        every time you hurt me it's like
                a knife pushing deeper into
my soul!

What did I do to deserve
        such pain in my
                life!

What happened to the person?
        I fall in love with!

Why do you always say
        you live me but all
                you show me is pain!

Sometimes I wished I never met you!

Painful Facts

You know what's more
            painful than
        death!
It's being alive and not
            having
        reason to be alive!

You know what's sadder
            than being
    betrayed!
Its not being able to trust
            again!

You know what's worse
            than being
    depressed!
It's loving too deep!

But, do you know
            what's more painful
        than loving someone!
It's not being loved back!

You know what hurt's
        more than
a bullet wound!
It's being used and played
            with, like a
    instrument!

You know what's horrible
        about life!
It's because it's not fair!

Painless

She's gone!
She has faded into
the darkness!

She lived with grief
but now she's
relief!

She feels no pain
and no
anxiety!

All those emotional
pains she felt
are now gone!

Those swollen red eyes,
from her tears are
no more!

The darkness swift away
her pain!
And left no trace of
her past!

$\mathcal{O}$ $\mathcal{B}$ $\mathcal{O}$

Pearl's Fear!!!

Let me tell you my
      deepest, darkest secret!
The thing I fear the most,
       more than rejection!

The thing that makes me
    toss and turn all night,
that one thing that
        can turn my whole world
upside down!

It keeps my brain active all
    day long!
      It makes me want to cry
at night!

To you it may be funny
      But to me
It's petrifying!

My biggest fear is my love, my heart,
   my piler, my friend, my mother,
      my, sister, my grandmother!

Peace

Peace in my heart is
like a calm
sea!

Peace brings gratification
and peace of
mind!

Peace brings family and friends
closer!

Peace is the best thing
that could ever
happen to
anyone!

Peace is like a blooming
Rose!

Peace brings glee and
satisfaction
to a
nation!

Perfect

Am I beautiful as
a diamond?

Does my body have
a shape?

Is my fashion taste
outstanding?

Do you think glasses
suite me?
Am I friendly to the
people around me?

Is my weight perfect
The way it is?

Why can't I stop asking
questions?

Am I perfect as I am!

Played

I loved you!

Who knew you were
playing me!

Who thought you were
capable of that!

Who would have wondered?
you were a
player!

I loved you!

You took my heart and
dragged it through
the mud!

You took all you could
get,
You played me like a
Video-game!

Poetry

Poetry helps me to connect
with my inner
beauty.
When Poetry is alive it makes
me alive.

It brings peace and love
in my life,
It helps me to embrace
my feelings!

Poetry is the essence
of my soul.

It gives me a better
        understanding!
Poetry is always their
            for me when the
    world has turned away from
                me!

It comforts me, it unlocks
        my chained heart!

Poetry is my beginning and
        my end!

Promised

You promised too never
go,
You promised to be there
for me!

But you lied!

You told me you'll
love me
Unconditionally!

You said you could
not live without
me!

But it was all an
act!

You played my heart
you used my love
against me!

You promised me happiness
and love!

But it was all a
lie!

𝒹 ℬ 𝒹

Questions?

I'm always asked the same
    questions every day!

Why do you like being
    alone?

Do you even have any
    friends?

Why do you love cutting
    yourself?

Why don't you stop hurting
    yourself?

Why are you so desperate
    for attention?

And I always get one statement!

If you really had depression you would
    be dead by now,

I only have two words to everyone
    "I'm tired"

Real Meaning

Love is fake, love is
          useless, love
    is worthless!

Love is weak, all it
     brings is tears, heartbreaks,
sadness and pain!

Love is a curse, that
       was placed in our
hearts!

The worst torture in
       life is love, it's pain
is sharper than a blade!

Love is a fancier word
      for pain, it's a
   nicer world for betrayal!

It tears your soul apart,
      it demolishes your trust leaving
  behind insecurity!

Love is a beautiful name for death!

Regret!

Can you see her,
Can you hear her,
Can you feel her?

Can you feel what she
    feels?
Can you see what she
    sees?
Can you hear what she
    hears?

No, you can't!

Did you feel her pain?
Did you hear the voices in
    her head?
Did you see the pain in her
    eyes?

Of course, you didn't!

Do you want to see her
    pain?
Do you want to feel her
    pain?
Definitely!

But, why *do* you want
    to see her pain?

When you're the course of
        the pain!

Why *do* you want to hear
    the voices in her
head?

When you're the reason they
        are there!

You could've been a friend but,
    decided to be a bully!

    Now live with the regret!

Remind Me

You don't have to remind
me!

I know, I don't have the
best body shape!

I know, I'm not the
prettiest!

I know, I'm not the
smartest person!

I know, I don't have any
friends!

I know, I'm useless as a
human being!

But most of all

I know, I'm worthless!

So, you don't have to remind
me every day!

Rewind and resume

Stop for a moment and
　　　rewind your memories!

Think of your pain and happiness
　　　and how far it has
　　bought you!

Think about the people who stuck
　　　by you through
　　thick and thin!

Think about your past and present
　　　and compare them, and
　　change them!

Think of the nights you cried
　　　yourself to sleep, those
　　days you wouldn't eat!

Think of those times were you
　　　would be over the moon,
and ask yourself why you're happy!
When you have thought of all those things
　　　and the course and the people!
You may resume with life!

Road Trip

No matter how much
>You can say "I love you"
If your actions say otherwise
>>just know there's no love!

No matter how much you can
>say 'sorry'
If it's not from the heart,
>It's like watering a dead plant!

No matter how much you can
>say "Please talk to me"
If you are always judgemental and
>>not supportive,
It's like a car that doesn't have petrol!

Life is a two-way road trip
>One road takes you to your destination
While the other one goes off the cliff!

>Think and choose your road
carefully!

Sadness

My smile is fake,
my laughter is forced!

My love has become,
hate!
My strength has been
taken away!

Sadness has taken over,
my whole body!

Sadness has always been
my fear, but
know my fear has become
my reality!

Sadness has taken everything and
everyone I loved,
away from me and,
Left me in
Grief!

Sadness is what I've,
become!
And will die with my sadness!

෪ ℬ ෪

Scars

I don't create scars
for decorations,
I create my scars
for memories,

I don't create scars
for attention,
I create my scars
for happiness,

I don't love creating
my scars but,
My scars make me happy!

My scars are what
make me stronger,
It creates my personality!

My scars are my
joy and happiness!

Season of friends

Friends are like the
seasons of
        the year!

One moment they're
        there, next
they're not!

One second they're
        with you
next they don't
        notice you!

Some days they're
        happy and sunny
while some days they're
                blue and dull!

Times they support you
        while at times
go against you!

True friends don't exist
        all they
        do is use you!

Set Free

I have set you free
 bye!
I have set you free
 my love!

Not because I wanted
 too,
Not because I had
 too!

I have set you free!

You once held the key
 to my life!
You once bought joy to
 my heart!

 But

I have set you free!
 to find
 happiness again!

Some

Some say I'm addicted
        well, I say I'm
                not!

Some say I want
        attention
well, I know I
            don't need it!

Some think I'm happy
        well, I know I'm
sad!

Some say she's just down
        well, I know
I'm depressed!

Some think I'm pretending
        if only they knew
I'm not!

Some think I have friends
        if only they knew
I'm actually alone!

If only knew me
        better than
                judging me!

Somethings

They are things in life,
not everyone should,
know!

Somethings in life are just,
meant to stay a,
secret!

They are things we shouldn't
even tell others!

Sometimes

Sometimes I feel my life is
like a train ride,
Sometimes I wish I can go
back in
time!

Sometimes I feel like a
paper drifting in
the wind!

Sometimes I wish I was never
born!

Sometimes my life is hard like
a rock!

Sometimes I feel like my life is
like a fan that is
spinning
around in circles!

But, sometimes will always be,
sometimes!

ॐ ॐ ॐ

Soul

I'm broken, not just
     my heart,
  but also, my soul!
I'm torn not just on
     the outside
        but also
     spiritually!

I'm damaged goods
     physically and
  emotionally!

I'm in piece's not just
      in my soul
    but also, in my
     inner-self!

I'm empty, I'm lost in
     my world of,
darkness!

See I loved her!
    she let me down
she broke my whole entire
      soul!

Suicide

I am a girl who doesn't
care about her
life!

I don't care what happen
to me cause,
I am useless
as a human!

I have tried committing
Suicide,
But I failed!

I have damaged my skin
with blades and
glasses!

I got tired of the blood,
so, I committed
suicide!

This time!

Speaking Up

I don't hurt myself
    because, I
enjoy doing it!

I don't isolate myself
    because, I
don't have friends!

I don't stop loving myself
    because, I'm
not beautiful!

I don't torture myself
    because, I
want attention!

I don't speak to
    because, I
want to be judged!

It's because,
I'm tired of wanting help!
I'm tired of being hurt!
I'm tired of being used!
    I'm tired of everything!

Take Me

Take me to the place
were theirs
peace!

Take me to the place
were I'll
be loved!

Take me to the place
where I call
home!

Take me to a place were
I will know myself!

Where I will feel no
pain!
Were I will be loved?
and were
there is peace!

Take me to the place were
I belong!

Thank You

Thank you, depression!
Thank you, haters!
Thank you, hard times!
Thank you, anxiety!
Thank you, fake friends!
Thank you, razor!
Thank you, heart breaker!
Thank you, admirers!
Thank you, love!
Thank you, failure!
Thank you, life!
Thank you, darkness!
Thank you, sadness!
Thank you, judgers!
Thank you, challenges!
Thank you, encouragers!
Thank you, loneliness!

But most of all Thank you to
everyone who tore me!
Thank you for everything!
And I'll continue saying Thank you!

The Day

The day I died
was the
end!

The day my heart
finally found
peace!

The day my mind
shut down to
sleep!

The day my body
become calm and
relaxed!

The day I finally
found my
inner peace!

The day I died
was the
happiest day!

A day I lost all emotions!

Too Many Questions! (TMQ)

Do you ever sit down and
    wish you were
 never born or even better
      never existed in the
Universe?

Do you ever ask yourself what
    you did to deserve
so much pain in your
    life?

Do you ever think about the reason?
    why you are
 surround with negativity and
     darkness!

And laugh that no matter how much
    you ask yourself those
 questions you never get answers for
    them!

Have you ever thought why sometimes?
you feel lonely and
useless to everyone around!

No matter how much you ask or
think, you will never
get your answers!

Truly

I truly miss you,
I truly do!

I truly love you,
with all my,
heart!

I never wanted to
leave,
I never wanted it
to end!

I want to come
back to your
loving heart!

I want to see your
smile and hear
your laughter like before!

Truth be Told

Cold, but not too
      cold!
Hot, but warm will
      do!

Love, is attractive but
hatred is addictive!

Fake friends are bought but
True friends are gained!

Happiness is rare but,
sadness is common!

Cold, but not too
      cold!
Hot, but warm will
      do!

Family is strength and
      love!
Friends are weakness and
      hate!

Cold, but not too
        cold!
Hot, but warm will
        do!

True Friend

I thought, I had
    found a sister
in you!

I thought, I finally
    found someone to
trust and love!

When I looked into your
    eyes, they sparkled
    with innocence!

Not knowing that behind
    that innocence
    laid a snake,
        waiting to show it's
    colourful scales!

When it finally immerged
    it left me speechless!

To have thought, I had
    found a true friend, more
like a true serpent!

Unconditional love

My love is beyond words
        it grows every
second!

Every time I hear your voice
        my heart
            accelerates!

My love is a train trip
        that has gotten me off the track!

My love is higher than the
        highest mountain!
It's deeper than the deepest
        waters!
It's wider than the widest
        ditch!

My love is like a flame that burns
        up cause of gasoline!
My love is more than I can
        describe in words but
can describe in actions!

My love is dangerous and
        contagious and is never
ending!

Unknown

There's beauty in everything
all you have to do is
observe carefully!

There's a mystery behind
the unknown
that only a few would know!

Everything and everyone
has a story to tell
just in a different way!

The small things can
end up being the most
Gorgeous thing!

Everyday holds a key
to a new dawn and
new adventures!

Everyone has had an experience
they'll never forget!

Just remember trying something
new can make you discover
hidden potential!

Useless

My life is useless,
I can't live like this,
Anymore!

My heart is filled with
scars and pain,
My breathe is painful when
I breath!
My eyes are redd from,
crying all the,
time!

I can't talk without me,
mumbling my
words!

My tears burn my eyes,
They sting me like,
I have been
stung by a
bee!

I was given a useless life!

War of soul

Her life was as peaceful
as a dove,
Her soul was as calm
as a sea
bed!

Her life was not all
peaceful!
Her soul was not calm
as the
sea bed!

Her life was a war
that was never
endless!
Her soul was restless
that didn't want
to be calm!

She struggled her way
out but,
failed!

Her spirit was quiet
       like a stone,
Her heart was cold
          and dark!

Her life was never
       peaceful!
And will never
       be peaceful!

Her spirit mislead
       her to the
wrong path!

Her soul failed to
          save
               her!

We

We don't talk these,
days!
I miss your charming
voice!

We don't look at each
other!
I miss your attractive
eyes!

We don't walk together
anymore!
I miss our long walks
together!
I feel distant from you!

When I see you

I am always blushing
when you appear,
You take my worries away
and replace it with a
smile!

When you look into my eyes
my heart melts,
You stole my heart when
I first me you!

You are my strength
You make me want to wake
up every day!

Why

Why do treat me
like rubbish?
I am human like you
and have feelings
like you?

Why do you fake that you
love me,
when you know that you
don't?

What did I ever do to
deserve your
unkindness?

I love you, but do
you love me?

Why

Why *do* you shut me,
out!
I only want to be your
friend, and love you!

Why *do* I feel like I,
don't belong!
Why *do* I feel like I,
am nothing!

Is it just me, or is
it you!

I *don't* know!

Why I cut

I don't cut cause I
love too,
I cut because it takes
the pain away!
That's why I cut!

I don't cut for
fun,
I cut cause it
calms me
down!

I don't enjoy seeing
My blood,
But it eases my
anxiety!

That's why I cut!

My cuts are my scars
My scars are my memory
My memory is my past!

That's why I cut!

Why I love you

I love you!
Not because of your looks,
No, but because of your
Heart!

You make me smile when I
am down,
You make me laugh when I
frown,

That's why I love
you!

You are always there for me
when I need you,
You treat me like a queen when I
feel like a princess!

That's why I love
you!

Words Hurt

Sticks and stones my break
my bones,
But your words don't break me
instead, they kill
me!

Your words pierce through my
heart like a sharp
spear!

Words may not kill me physically
but they kill me
Emotionally and mentally!

Your words always replay in my
mind which drives
me nuts!

Your mouth is the gun your words
are the bullet!
When you speak your words
come shooting at me!

Your words hurt that
I will never forget
them!

Why love!

Why should I love!
    When I can't
Why should I care!
    When you don't!

What is love to
    me!
Why can't I love
    people!

Why should I smile
when it's just fake!
What is the meaning
    of friendship?

Nobody loves me so
    why must I
love them!

All my friends pretend
    so why can't
        I!

Why should I force
   when I don't
       fit in!

Why should I love?

Worst Nightmare

You laid there like you were
frozen!
You had no smile plastered,
you were silent with
no movement!

For a moment I thought
you would wake-up
and say I love you my
baby-girl!

But! That's when reality hit
me!
You were gone, never to hear
you say my baby-girl,
never to hear your voice!

You fell into an eternal sleep that
you will never wake-up
from!

I thought it was a nightmare in
my head, but actually
it was my worst nightmare in
reality!

Years

Five years old:
happy, care free, loving
When will I grow up?

Ten years old:
Naughty, fake friends, hard working
Why am I still young?

Sixteen years:
scars, suicidal, makeup, boyfriend,
popularity, poor marks
Why was I born?

Eighteen years old:
Alcohol, weed, parties, clubs,
left school
How did I get here?

Twenty-one years old:
Pregnant, no-education, poverty
Why didn't I listen?

You

You are different in your
own way,
And that's what makes
you unique!

You are the sweetest person
I have met,
You are very special to me,
You treat people with
tenderness,
You help those around
You,

You are a good friend that
people love,
You respect your friends and
classmates!

That's why you are different
And unique to
Me!

You are beautiful

You are the most beautiful,
thing anyone has
seen!

Your beauty blinds people around
You,
Your beauty makes people faint
when you pass by!
You are so beautiful like the
brightest star in
the sky!

You are so beautiful that you
put the flowers
out of business!

You are beautiful like a rainbow
after a rainy
day!

You killed her

They was a girl in my class,
she was very quiet and
kind!

She was always bullied by
a group of
boys!

She was called names, pushed
around and they would
also take her
things!

Little did they know that she
was cutting herself,
day after day!

They words broke her into pieces,
she got tired
of life!

So, she committed suicide cause
of the pain!

Your

Your smile is like a
thief,
Your eyes pierce through
mine when,
you look at me!

Your love is the size of the
Galaxies,
Your love for me is unconditional
that it drives me,

Your heart is what tells, me
you're the one for,
me!

❦ ℬ ❦

Your Heart

Your heart is made of
gold,
Your heart is like a
Rose Quartz
Stone!

Your heart attracts everyone's
love around you!
Your heart gains people's
trust!

Your heart shines brighter than
a diamond ring!
Your heart is bigger than a
60 carat diamond!

Your heart is what creates
your love!

Your words

Your words hurt me, to this
day I haven't
forgotten them!

But your words also made me
Stronger,
They built a warrior out of
me!

You thought your words tore
me apart but,
You were wrong they gave me
power!

Look at me now, I have
become an,
Almighty ninja because of your
words!

Your words didn't take away
my self-esteem,
Your words improved my self-
esteem!

Printed in the United States
By Bookmasters